Farm-Raised

DEVOTIONALS

Ida Mae Couch

ISBN 978-0578-47488-5

Bible scripture NIV unless otherwise noted
Cover design by Ida Mae Couch and Aubry Couch

Printed in the United States of America
Published by Lobry Publishing

You can reach Ida Mae at:
LobryPublishing@gmail.com

Or on Instagram
@ lobrypublishing

To my parents,
Joe and Joyce Walton

Contents

Contents

Where It All Began

My parents met in a cotton patch in rural Arkansas back in the 1950s. Several years after they married, they took over my grandparents' small farm. It was about 18 acres in size.

In order to be a stay-at-home mom for my siblings and me, my mom took care of growing cotton. Dad would plant it, and Mom would take care of keeping weeds out, and then picking it...with help from us kids. It was hard work.

I have lots of memories of going out in the field with my Mom. I had a big straw hat to protect my face and shoulders from the sun. I would walk up and down the rows of cotton plants as my mom did her work. Our cats would come out to the field with us too, and lay in the cool dirt.

In late summer, when it was pickin' time, Mom hand-picked the cotton. Her cotton sack had a long strap on it, and she wore it like it was a large purse. Her cotton sack would slowly grow to be a stuffed pillow. I remember riding her cotton-filled sack when I got tired. I would sit on it as she dragged it down the rows of cotton.

Just as plants need tending in order to grow and flourish, we also need to tend to ourselves. If we don't, we'll risk being taken over by the "weeds." When we keep the "weeds" out, then we can grow and produce good quality fruits.

We can still produce when weeds are around us, but we won't be as productive. The product quality may possibly be affected too. Weeds will choke out the goodness by robbing us of vital spiritual nutrients that will give a higher yield. It's important to keep as many of the weeds away as possible.

"Above all else, guard your heart, for everything you do flows from it." Proverbs 4:23

Mom, It's Chasing Me!!!

It was one of those hot, sunny days in the cotton field with Mom and the cats. I had wandered off a row or two from where Mom was working. I bent down to look at something, and when I looked up, I saw a HUGE bird coming at me. It was as big as me! At least it seemed that way to my 3 or 4-year-old eyes. I hollered, "Mom! It's chasing me!" She came to my rescue with a bit of a chuckle. "It's just a killdeer. You probably got too close to her nest."

Just a killdeer? JUST A KILLDEER? Does that mean it's big enough to kill a deer??? All I knew was that it was big and it was after me.

I called out to my mom because I knew that she would protect me no matter what was chasing me. She would have stood between me and whatever harm was coming my way. All I had to do was call her name.

God's like that. He offers security and protection. Just as my mom was right there; a holler away, God is too.

"...call on me in the day of trouble; I will deliver you, and you will honor me." Psalm 50:15

"I love those who love me. And those who diligently seek me will find me." Proverbs 8:17 NASB

Yes, God is just a holler away, or as close as a whisper.

Weights and Standards

When harvest time came for cotton, it was a busy time. All five of us would be out in the field hand-picking the cotton and filling our sacks. When the sack was full it would be weighed. Dad would keep track of how much was picked so he would know about how much money he would get for the crop.

I remember my dad hanging an empty sack from the cotton scale and he would sit me in it like I was sitting in a swing to see how much I weighed. That was a fun time.

Weights and measures have standards that were put in place in order to be fair in our trading. These are man-made standards that help us establish value.

There are other standards that we use in our culture that are a bit more obscure, but they can still have value and affect our perceptions. We measure someone's knowledge by grades and diplomas. We evaluate certain items by the materials from which they are made or the company that manufactured them. Some brands are better than others. Some schools are more rigorous than others. But it all boils down to man's idea of value.

Man's ideas are just that; man's ideas. How God views you is the real standard. It's easy to psych ourselves out and say, "Well, I'm not smart enough to do..." or "I'm not good enough to..." Whose measuring stick are you using? If God has something to be accomplished, He will give you what you need to accomplish it. It's not about what some diploma says or what your bank account has to offer. We all hold value in God's eyes. We are all precious to Him.

"Are not five sparrows sold for two pennies? Yet not one of them is forgotten by God. Indeed, the very hairs on your head are all numbered. Don't be afraid; you are worth more than many sparrows."
Luke 12: 6-7

Pink Sippy Cup

My sippy cup… It was pretty special to me. It was pink and plastic and had lots of teeth marks on the spout where I had sunk my teeth into it. Every morning at breakfast, Mom would fill it up, and I would sip on it until it was empty. Then she would fill it again whenever I asked which was likely several times a day.

There's a story in John 4 that you're likely familiar with, about something called "living water." Let's look at it with fresh eyes:

(paraphrased) Jesus went to a well and a woman came to draw water. He asked her for a drink, but she was a bit stunned that he was even talking to her because she was a Samaritan and Jews didn't associate with Samaritans. He mentioned something about "living water" to her and of course, she didn't understand. Water isn't something we

consider to be alive. He went on to explain that with this water she would never be "thirsty" again. She was ready to know more about this "living water." Pulling water out of the ground was a lot of hard work.

It's important to see that scripture says it was about noon. We assume she came later in the day to avoid the crowds possibly because she was not "acceptable" to others in the town due to the lifestyle she was living. She waited to do this chore until no one would be there to harass her or shame her with their looks.

If this had been me, I think I would have been defensive toward Jesus. First of all, He's a Jewish man and He shouldn't be talking to her. Then He starts talking about some sort of living water that will keep her from ever being thirsty again. I think I would have felt like He was trying to take advantage of me.

Of course, we see it from this side of history and know Jesus was being careful because He could easily scare her away. He subtly told her who He was and soon her eyes were opened and she knew without a doubt who He truly was. She left her water jar there to go back into the town to tell others about Jesus.

We have access to this same "living water." It pours freely. We can fill our "sippy cup" with all the goodness that God has to offer. I encourage you to sip often.

Old House, New House

The first house I lived in was (as we so affectionately called it) the "old house." It was a small, 2-bedroom house, and it had been given to my parents by a family friend. It had been a house located in town, and my parents had it relocated to the farm.

I have a few vague memories of the old house such as sitting at the kitchen table with my pink, plastic sippy cup with the chewed-up and teeth-dented spout. I remember caring for a runt pig on the back porch that had been rejected by her mother, and I remember a grapevine in the backyard. The juicy Concord grapes were a seasonal treat. I can remember how creaky and uneven the floors were, too, because the house had been uprooted from its foundation in town.

The "old house" was never meant to be the permanent home for us. Mom and dad knew they wanted to build a house eventually, and in the spring of 1970, the new house construction began.

I remember the foundation being placed. There were cement blocks getting stacked with mortar in between. There was a BIG sand pile (heaven to a young child) where I could play with my big brother's digging toys. Later on, there would be small blocks of wood to stack to pretend I was building a house for my dolls.

After a few months, the house was completed. Move in day was my mom's birthday. What better gift could she possibly get than a lovely new home! My sister, who was only 10, baked Mom a cake in the brand-new oven. It was a very special day.

One of the stories I listened to in Sunday school was about two different houses being built. We even had a song that we sang about it.

"Therefore, everyone who hears these words of mine and puts them into practice is like a wise man who built his house on a rock. The rain came down and the streams rose, and the winds blew and beat against that house; yet it did not fall because it had its foundation on the rock. But everyone who hears these words of mine and does not put them into practice is like a foolish man who built his house on the sand. The rain came down, the streams rose, and the winds blew and beat against that house, and it fell with a great crash." Matthew 7:24-27

Our "new house" was definitely more solidly constructed in the physical sense, but even in the "old house" that was a little rickety, we lived on the firm foundation of Jesus's words. Our home was filled with love for God, and love for others.

That pink sippy cup with all the teeth marks on the spout disappeared when we moved. I don't know what happened to it. I looked and looked for it in the new house, but I never found it. When I shared this memory with my mom, she had a suspicious look on her face.

The Playhouse

Not long after we moved, Mom and Dad began a
little building project just a few feet from the house.
It began with a small concrete pad. Walls were built
around the perimeter and I realized they were
building a playhouse for me! How excited I was
because I loved playing "house." Soon the walls
were completed and a roof topped it off. There was a
place for a door, but there were no windows and I felt
my playhouse needed windows. Every playhouse
had windows!

I would spend hours in my bedroom pretending
that I was a busy little momma baking in an
imaginary kitchen. I cared for my imaginary babies
as I would put them in their highchair and feed them.

I would rock them in my little rocking chair and lay them in their beds. Now, I was going to have a whole playhouse of my very own with a real kitchen, and room for more babies!

I would tell my mom and dad how I couldn't wait for them to get it finished so I could play in it. They would laugh and tell me it wasn't for me, but I knew they were just trying not to make it so obvious. They wanted to surprise me and they would tell me it was a pump house. Well, I didn't know what a pump house was, so that must have been some sort of code to make me think it was something else.

Yes, they were building a playhouse just for me!

Once the construction was completed, they started filling it with shovels, rakes, and all kinds of other tools. Why were they putting their things in my playhouse? If they kept putting their stuff in there, I wouldn't have room for my kitchen and baby beds. What were they thinking?!

As you can guess, I was pretty deflated by their taking over my space. It seemed mean to me that they had built this sweet cottage for me only to fill it up with their stuff.

Eventually, reality busted my delusional bubble. The space was truly never meant to be mine. My parents were speaking truth to me when they told me it was going to be a pump house. They tried earnestly to get me to understand and believe that, but my mind refused to believe what they were telling me. I was too caught up in my own thinking.

Jesus had a similar problem with the Pharisees. He tried to explain who He was to them, but they didn't believe it.

"How long will you keep us in suspense? If you are the Messiah, tell us plainly." Jesus answered, "I did tell you, but you do not believe." John 10: 24-25

Jesus would point to scripture where it had been prophesied about him. He performed miracles. He spoke in parables and even spoke truth directly to them, but many of them refused to believe.

There is another side to this story starting in verse 41 where not all were blinded by their own understanding:

"…and many people came to Him. They said, 'Though John never performed a sign, all that John said about this man was true.' **And in that place many believed in Jesus.**" (emphasis mine)

Our eyes can be opened to truth, if *we* are open to see truth.

Floor Furnace

In our new house, we had a gas furnace in the floor.
It had a metal grate over the top that looked like a
grid. It was in the middle of the walkway to the
living room, the kitchen, to the hallway that went to
the bathroom and our bedrooms. You HAD to walk
past it to go anywhere in the house.

I was scared to death of that furnace. I was only 3
when we moved into that house, and my parents had
put great emphasis on the importance of not letting
anything fall down into it. If paper fell into it the
house would catch on fire. Nothing was to be set on
it because it would melt and be destroyed. Do not
step on it or your feet will get burned. So, you can
imagine how my 3-year-old mind dealt with the
dangers there. That furnace was like a fire breathing
dragon, and you didn't want to wake it or make it
angry!

I have many memories of close calls with that beast. I remember I woke up one morning and one of the rules was being broken! The morning newspaper was covering the grate. The delivery person had mistakenly thrown it in the ditch and the newspaper was soaked. Mom and Dad had laid the paper over the furnace to dry it out so they could read it. I was filled with panic and couldn't understand this, but Mom and Dad assured me it was all under control and the house would not burn down.

Well, when they went to get the mostly-dried newspaper off the grate, a little piece of the newspaper was stuck to it. It was a tiny piece, but I freaked out. I just knew the house was going to burn down. Mom got the tweezers and plucked the paper scrap from the grate and all was safe again.

Another time, my dad had placed his dress shoes at the edge of the grate. He left them there a little too long and the rubber soles melted a little. Well, once again, panic filled me. That "dragon" was going to be so angry! The house was going to burn down for certain this time.

My understanding of God when I was little was kind of like my relationship with that furnace. I was afraid of it, and I was afraid of God. I didn't want to do the wrong thing or He'd get angry and I would be destroyed.

I've since learned that God is merciful, kind, and gives grace. He's not an angry, mean God, but a loving father who cares for me. When I realized that, it changed me. It took the fear away. Instead of looking at my mistakes and feeling worthless, I learned to look at my mess ups as opportunities to improve.

"...we have peace with God through our Lord Jesus Christ, through whom we have gained access by faith into this grace in which we now stand."
Romans 5: 1-2

I'll Be Good…

My mother would take me shopping with her to the grocery store, and to regular retail stores. In order for her to accomplish her tasks, she needed me to obey her and respect her rules as well as the rules of the store. My mother's rules were simple: stay with her, don't touch anything without asking first, and don't be loud. If I wasn't obedient, there was a flimsy plastic belt in the car that would be used on my behind. It truly was flimsy and would not have hurt a fly. It *would* hurt my pride though and would make me think twice about misbehaving again.

Another place I was given boundaries was when we went to worship. I was expected, even as a small child, to sit still and be quiet. I often took a baby doll to church to hold and love on during worship. Mom would also keep paper and pencil in her purse for me to keep me occupied. I was expected to stay seated and not cause distractions to those around us. If I didn't stick to the rules, there were consequences. I would be taken out of worship, taken outside and swatted on the leg…not hard, but just enough pain to make me think twice before I misbehaved again.

I actually remember the last time my mother took me out. I had been turning around and making faces at some people behind me. She warned me once to stop. When I did it again, I realized I had gone too far. I remember trying to change her mind and pleading with her on the way out. "I'll be good. Don't take me out. I'll be good." I made sure everyone in that building heard me too, but it didn't change her resolve. She took me out the back door of the auditorium and popped my leg. She made her point. She had expectations of me, and if I didn't adhere to those expectations there would be consequences. As I said, that was the last time she took me out. It finally clicked; be good, or else…

I don't think God is pointing His finger at us and saying, "Be good, or else…" He is patient with us. He gives us free rein to make our own choices. But God is a God of boundaries, and He will allow us to feel the pain of discipline when we step outside those lines.

"We know that in all things God works for the good of those who love him, who have been called according to his purpose." Romans 8:28

My mom needed me to respect her and listen to her. The world is full of dangers. By setting the limits, and setting them in my early years, I was less likely to get into trouble. I wanted to please my mom by adhering to her rules. That was the way I showed her love.

This is also the way we show God our love.

The Weekly Menu

My mom was a woman of routine and rituals. She assigned tasks to each day of the week, and this is how she kept her life and our home running smoothly.

Part of her routine was around meals. Each day had a meal assigned to it. This was our typical menu:

Sunday—roast beef with potatoes and carrots. (This cooked in the oven while we attended worship services.)

Monday--beans and cornbread

Tuesday—pork chops, fried potatoes, green beans, biscuits

Wednesday—hamburgers and French fries

Thursday—ham, potatoes (choice of mashed, fried, or soup), corn, biscuits

Friday—spaghetti

Sat—was "eat out" night (sometimes)

There were a few options here and there, but this was pretty regular.

By having a set menu, Mom knew how much groceries would cost, it made her grocery shopping simple, and we knew what to expect each evening.

I remember someone in the family getting tired of having roast every Sunday and complaining of having the same thing all the time. It's true. Routines can be good, but there is a downside as well. Boredom can set in. We get tired of doing the same thing over and over, week after week. Dissatisfaction leads to grumbling.

Numbers 11:4-6 tells about some complaints regarding a lack of meat. What's interesting in this particular setting is that it didn't start with the Israelites. It started with some "worthless foreigners." Yes, that is a quote from scripture.

"One day some worthless foreigners among the Israelites became greedy for food, and even the Israelites themselves began moaning, 'We don't have any meat! In Egypt, we could eat all the fish we wanted, and there were cucumbers, melons, onions, and garlic. But we're starving out here, and the only food we have is this manna'."

Now, I want you to put yourself in God's shoes for just a moment. Your children, the ones you chose to rescue from slavery, the ones you love SO much, are throwing a fit because (hear this in a whining tone),

"All I have is manna." (boo hoo hoo) "We don't have any meat!" (Pouty face with a foot stamp.)

How would you feel if your offspring became so ungrateful? I'm sure if you have children you have actually experienced this at least once. You wonder where your sweet, precious child went because this cannot be coming out of your sweet, precious child's mouth, right?

I offer you a dare. I dare you to go for a minute without complaining. Okay, maybe that's not challenging enough. Then try 15 minutes. How about 30? Or for an hour? Or a day? Could you go a whole day without complaining? If we can learn to turn the perspective toward God and hear ourselves the way we hear our children, we might be able to at least cut down our complaints. It's a start. It's not about tearing ourselves down because we fail so often. It's about changing and adjusting our attitude and perspective. It's a way to humble ourselves.

"Humble yourselves in the sight of the Lord, and He will lift you up." James 4:10

Being Told "No"

I've told you about my mom's routine, organized life. Part of the routine was Wednesday grocery shopping. She and I would head to town and go to Piggly Wiggly to get groceries for the week.

As I grew a little older, I was given some freedom to go through the store on my own. I wandered one day into an area where paper and pencils were shelved. This became my favorite place to go because they *sometimes* had paper doll books in this area. They didn't always have these so it was a real find if they were there. I LOVED paper dolls. (Still do.)

As well as being a woman of routine, my mother was also a serious money manager. For one thing, we didn't have much of it, and what we did have needed to be used for practical purposes.

On one particular visit, I remember finding a new stack of paper doll books. Oh! The thrill! I looked at each and every book. I picked the one I liked the best and went to find my mom to ask her if we could get it. I hoped against hope that she would say yes. As with most kids, I liked to get things and being told no was unpleasant and disappointing. I never knew what my mom's answer would be because sometimes it was yes, but more often it was no. But because the answer was sometimes yes, I had hope.

That's kind of how it is when we ask God for things. The hope is there just waiting for an answer. We hope it will be the answer we want.

One thing I've come to understand is that God is holy through and through. There is no evil or wrong in Him. (I John 1:5) Whatever He allows is good, no matter how awful it may appear to my human eyes. He is always right. I may not like His answer, but part of being His child is trusting that He is in control, and He knows best.

May your will align with God's will. That's what's important.

Mrs. Gleghorn

We had a neighbor who was a widow, and her name was Mrs. Gleghorn. She lived in a sweet little house across the road from us, and she didn't drive. I remember Mom taking her to town a few times when I was little so she could get groceries and supplies.

Back in those days, we didn't wear seat belts and kids didn't sit in car seats. My usual place in the car was standing in the middle of the front seat.

I remember a particular trip to town with Mrs. Gleghorn where I stood in the front seat in my usual spot. I had just learned how to whistle, and I was whistling up a storm. Mrs. Gleghorn was a bit disturbed by my new-found talent and got quite agitated that my mom was allowing me to continue my music making. She had a phrase that she started touting that went like this:

"Whistling girls and crowing hens always come to some bad end."

She grew up in a time when it was not proper for girls to whistle. I wasn't doing anything wrong by whistling, but because Mrs. Gleghorn believed it was inappropriate, it would be courteous and respectful for me to refrain from doing so while she was in our company.

"Be careful, however, that the exercise of your rights does not become a stumbling block to the weak." 1 Corinthians 8:9

One of the fruits of the spirit is self-control. I need to be considerate of how I behave and what I say because I am a reflection of God in all that I do. I'm learning to tell myself that just because I can, doesn't mean I should.

Party Line

When I think back to how things were in my childhood and compare them to our world today, I am amazed at the technology we have. The way we communicate is one of the most drastic changes, I think. In my lifetime we've gone from phones that dial, to phones with push-buttons, to cordless phones, to phones with answering machines, to cell phones. We don't even have to call someone to talk to them now. We just text a quick message. Let me take you back to a time more primitive.

When we moved into the "new" house, my parents had to be frugal to make ends meet. That $68 house payment was a lot back in the early '70s. Any way they could make a dollar stretch, they did it. One of the ways was having a "party line." How many of you know what that is? A party line, in my day, was a phone line with multiple family phones all funneled down to the same landline. Each family had their own phone number, but conversations could be heard in anyone's home when they picked up the phone receiver.

You can imagine the struggles a party line could (and did) cause. If you needed to use the phone, but your neighbor was on a call, you had to wait until the neighbor got off the phone. Private conversations could be overheard easily. Eavesdropping and gossip were big problems especially in a small town like ours. There was a certain etiquette that was supposed to be observed with party lines, but not everyone was cooperative. It caused quite a bit of stress in our home.

No one enjoys having other people "in their business." God knew that this would be a problem and set some boundaries in place, or at least the idea of boundaries.

"Do not spread false reports. Do not help a guilty person by being a malicious witness." Exodus 23:1

"Those who consider themselves religious and yet do not keep a tight rein on their tongues deceive themselves, and their religion is worthless." James 1:26

"With their mouths the godless destroy their neighbors, but through knowledge the righteous escape." Proverbs 11:9

"A perverse person stirs up conflict, and a gossip separates close friends." Proverbs 16:28

If we break it down, gossip is just one of those ugly tools we use when we want to feel better about ourselves. The "golden rule" applies here too. Treat others the way you want to be treated. Don't gossip if you don't want others gossiping about you. If this is something you struggle with, I encourage you to pray about it. Can you imagine a world without gossip?

After several months of trying to cope with a party line, my parents decided a private line would solve a lot of problems and eliminate some stress. My mom was quite pleased to have her privacy back.

Mud Pies

Springtime on the farm meant plowing and disking up the soil to prepare it for planting. I loved freshly plowed soil. I loved walking barefoot in it, and seeing my foot prints in it (until I stepped on a stem from last year's crop. OUCH! That hurt!) I liked scooping it up in my hands and letting it fall through my fingers. I liked the color too; a deep, rich, earthy brown.

I remember making mud pies and all sorts of other imaginative goodies this time of year too. I would borrow some of Mom's plastic containers from her kitchen cabinets. I would take them outside and fill them with some of that fresh-turned dirt and add a little bit of water from the water hose. Sticks were my utensils to stir the mixture together to create a nice, thick, brown, gooey mud. I'd then scoop up that glob and pretend to make cakes, cookies, pies, or whatever happened to be on my make-believe menu at that time.

When all my "cooking" was complete, I would have dirt and mud under all my fingernails, clumps of mud stuck between my fingers, and my palms would be smeared with brown muck. There wasn't a crevice in my hand that didn't have microscopic granules of dirt compressed into them. It took some serious scrubbing to get all that dirt off. I'd get the big stuff off outside at the water hose and then go inside to use soap to complete the cleaning. Even after using soap, there would sometimes still be areas that were sort of stained. It didn't matter how much I scrubbed, there were still brown areas.

"Getting our hands dirty" is an expression we use figuratively to mean we are going to dive into a job or project and make things happen. "Dirty hands" represents effort, productivity, hard work. It's a good thing.

Spiritually speaking, are you getting your hands dirty? This is not meant as a guilt trip, just food for thought. If your answer is "yes," good! Keep up the good work and keep growing! If your answer is "no," don't beat yourself up. Guilt is not a fruit of the Spirit. Do take some time and make some effort to turn your "no" into "yes". Whatever your age or season of life, there are always opportunities for God to use your abilities.

"Whatever you do, work at it with all your heart, as working for the Lord, not for men, since you know that you will receive an inheritance from the Lord as a reward. It is the Lord Christ you are serving."
Colossians 3:23-24

Grandma's Stay

Growing cotton was hard work, and the pay wasn't great. My mom decided she needed to go back to school so that she could have a job that was a bit more stable and predictable. I had one more year before I was to start school, so this presented a dilemma; who was going to take care of me? My grandmother agreed to help for the nine months that Mom would be attending a nursing school.

Grandma didn't live too far away, but it wasn't going to work for her to drive back and forth every day. So, Mom and Dad moved a twin bed into the bedroom my sister and I shared. Our room wasn't big so another bed in there took up a lot of room, but we made it work. I remember her bed looking so sweet with one of her quilts laying on top.

Grandma and I were constant companions. She would read to me, fix my lunch, take me on her errand runs; whatever she needed to do I was there tagging along.

Sometimes she would take me shopping at the mall. I didn't enjoy going to the mall. It was a big place. It required a lot of walking and standing. It wore my little legs out, but Grandma knew how to cajole me.

In the entrance to one of the department stores, there was a self-serve candy kiosk and it had all kinds of different candies. Grandma would fill 2 little bags; one with chocolate twist drops, and one with white-chocolate twist drops. This is where my love for white chocolate began. It was so decadent melting in my mouth. It was creamy and smooth tasting. To this day whenever I get white chocolate, my mind goes back to these early, childhood moments.

As Christians, we anticipate the reward of Heaven. Jesus told his apostles that there was a special place being prepared.

"My father's house has many rooms; if that were not so, would I have told you that I am going there to prepare a place for you? And if I go and prepare a place for you, I will come back and take you to be with me that you may also be where I am. You know the way to the place where I am going." John 14:2-4

There are descriptions in Revelation chapter 21 of this beautiful place. Some of the descriptions there tell us that it is a city of pure gold with precious stones for the foundations and gates of pearls.

Not only is it a beautiful place, but we're told there will be no pain or sadness there. Our legs won't get tired from walking and standing. We won't be hungry or thirsty.

"Never again will they hunger; never again will they thirst. The sun will not beat down on them, nor any scorching heat. For the Lamb at the center of the throne will be their shepherd; he will lead them to springs of living water. And God will wipe away every tear from their eyes." Rev 7:16-17

"He will wipe every tear from their eyes. There will be no more death or mourning or crying or pain, for the old order of things has passed away." Rev 21:4

The next time you feel tired and discouraged, remember that God has a treat waiting just for you. It will be a million times better than the best tasting chocolate.

Finicky and Particular

I've shared about my mother working the cotton field so she could be a stay-at-home mom. She was the only person that had taken care of me, and the way she had done things was all I had known.

When Grandma came and stayed with us so that Mom could go to school, I quickly learned that there was more than one way to do certain things, such as making a peanut butter jelly sandwich. My mom had always put peanut butter on one slice of bread and jelly on the other. Then she put the two bread slices together to form the sandwich.

One day, Grandma started making a sandwich for me for lunch. I watched as she put the peanut butter on one slice, but then...THEN she put jelly ON TOP OF THE PEANUT BUTTER!!! WHAT WAS SHE DOING?!?! That's not how a peanut butter jelly sandwich was made! It was all ruined! I tried to explain to her in my panic that she was doing it wrong...all wrong. That wasn't the way my mom did it. It wasn't going to taste right. I came unglued (in as nice a way as my 5-year-old self could).

My poor grandmother was perplexed. What had she done that was so wrong and different to cause this reaction? I mean, a peanut butter jelly sandwich is hard to mess up, right? But in my eyes, it was destroyed. You weren't supposed to put the jelly on top of the peanut butter!

Grandma explained to me that it really didn't matter which order or how the 2 ingredients got put on the sandwich, it was the end result that mattered.

So, I conceded through my tears. I took a bite of the sandwich and sure 'nough! It tasted just like the ones my mom made. I was relieved and delighted.

Another example of havoc in the kitchen was one morning when she asked me what I wanted for breakfast. I said, "Ceralmilk." (pronounced sear'-ral-milk)

"What kind?" Grandma asked.

"Ceralmilk!" I said again.

"What kind?" Grandma asked a bit more perturbed this time.

"Ceralmilk!" I exclaimed. I mean, what other kind is there? You put cereal in a bowl with some sugar, pour milk over it and it's "ceralmilk."

"What kind of cereal do you want?" Grandma clarified.

There was more than one kind??!! This was news to me. I only knew of the white box with the rooster shape on the front holding a bowl of corn flakes.

That was when I had the awakening that "ceralmilk" meant cereal and milk. You could put different kinds of cereal in a bowl and pour milk over it. I had been enlightened! It didn't mean I wanted to stray from my usual blend of corn flakes, sugar, and milk, but I was finally able to communicate what I wanted to my grandma.

My grandma and I had to work through our frustrations of learning to communicate with each other in those first few days of me being in her care. It doesn't seem like it should have been so difficult. We both spoke English, but because I was so young, I had very limited experience with communicating my needs.

"Be completely humble and gentle; be patient, bearing with one another in love." Ephesians 4:2

Grandma was pretty patient with me. We may have been frustrated with each other, but she kept working to understand me because she loved me and wanted to take care of me.

I've Run Out of Juice

Yes, I was Grandma's constant companion. She took me everywhere with her, even the funeral home. As a small child, I felt out of place there. There weren't any other kids to play with. All the adults were being kind of quiet. They were dressed in their "Sunday best." It wasn't Sunday, and this wasn't worship. This felt like a strange place.

Funerals are sad. That's just a fact. It doesn't matter if you know the person or not; it's sad. At this funeral with my grandmother, my very young heart was touched...deeply. I began to cry. Grandma handed me a tissue. She also handed me a piece of gum. I unwrapped it, set the wrapper aside, and folded the stick of gum into my mouth. It was so juicy and full of flavor. I didn't feel the need to cry when I had the gum to distract me. But soon the gum lost its flavor. "I've run out of juice," I'd whisper to Grandma. That was the explanation I gave when the gum didn't taste good anymore. So, Grandma would give me another piece. Well, it also ran out of flavor, and I asked for another piece. I don't know how many pieces of gum I went through, but Grandma eventually said she was out of gum.

The "juice" in the gum had distracted me from the unpleasant circumstance of being in a sad place with sad people over a sad circumstance. I know of folks who prefer to live in a world of distractions. It's easier than facing whatever is really in front of them.

"...watch yourselves lest your hearts be weighed down with dissipation and drunkenness and cares of this life, and that day comes upon you suddenly like a trap." Luke 21:34 ESV

Dissipation means to squander money, energy or resources.

We can spend a lot of time, energy, money, etc. when we are trapped in distractions, or when we avoid facing what is really keeping us stuck. I went through a whole pack of gum!

"Taste and see that the Lord is good; blessed is the one who takes refuge in Him." Psalm 34:8

Grandma Took a Break

Many of my grandma's siblings settled in the St Louis area. She would take a bus trip to go visit them from time to time.

During her time of staying with us, she decided to take one of these trips. I'm certain she was torn between getting away for a few days and caring for me (wink wink). (I'm also certain she needed the break.)

During her absence, other arrangements were made for me. I would spend the days with an older cousin. I think she was keeping other kids too. I don't remember too many details about it. The one thing I do remember is she didn't have Kool-Aid. That was my beverage of choice. Instead, she had grapefruit juice. I had never had grapefruit juice. I had tasted grapes and I liked grape juice, so grapefruit juice

51

sounded really yummy. I took a big gulp of that pretty, coral-pink beverage…and thought I was going to throw up. YUCK! All I could think was "BITTER!" I tried to be respectful of my cousin. I know she thought she was giving me something good, but that was the absolute worst thing I had ever put in my mouth. After lunch, she told me I needed to finish my drink, but that was not going to happen.

The name of this juice and the pretty color was deceptive. Because I associated "grapefruit" with "grapes" and "grape juice" I had an impression that it would be tasty. The color also was alluring; pretty coral must equal yummy flavor, right? No.

Satan enjoys fooling us. He deceives us by taking something we know and changes it just the slightest bit. Or maybe it's something attractive and seems harmless, and we think, "Oh, that seems fine. There's nothing there that can be bad," and before we know it, we're trapped.

It's very easy to get deceived. It really is. It doesn't take much to get us off track.

In 2 Corinthians 11:13-15, Paul says, "For such men are false apostles, deceitful workers, masquerading as apostles of Christ. And no wonder, for Satan masquerades himself as an angel of light. It is not surprising, then, if his servants also masquerade as servants of righteousness. Their end will be what their actions deserve."

That day at my cousin's house, I learned that things are not always as good as they appear. I did not drink grapefruit juice ever again after that day; never...ever. Nope.

Oops! I Got Caught

My sister and I are complete opposites and we had to share a room when we were growing up. She is a few years older than me so you can imagine the grief I caused in her world. She never had a room to herself...never. She had to share a room with our brother before she shared one with me.

Even though we were sisters occupying the same space, there were certain things that were off limits to me. I was envious of some of my sister's things. She had a really cool dollhouse and she fixed it up so cute. My instructions were to "leave it alone." Well, being the stinker-of-a-little-sister I was, I *had* to play with it. While she was at school, I would play with the dolls and have a wonderful time of pretending.

Several days went by where I played with it, and she never knew because I always put everything back the way it was.

One day I forgot to put things back in their places. She came home and saw that I had been in her stuff. She. Was. Not. Happy. My secret was out, and soon my tail would be blazing because of my dishonesty.

As I looked back on this situation, I realized that I wasn't sorry for being disobedient. I was sorry I had been caught. It was something I was doing on a regular basis, and I felt I had the right to go beyond my sister's wishes to play with her stuff. I would have continued in my sneaky ways if I hadn't been found out.

"Your sin will find you out." Numbers 32:23

Yes, I was found out. I was punished, too. My heart was not sorry for what I had done at the time, but I gained respect for my sister's property. I never played with my sister's dollhouse again without permission.

Practice, Practice, Practice

When you were a kid did you have things that you practiced such as piano, guitar, or some other musical instrument? Maybe you played ball or practiced some other type of sport. There are some of us that practiced other things; more practical things like...practicing getting on the school bus.

For the first few years of my school career, I, indeed, practiced this feat every summer about a week before school was to begin. I had to prepare how I was going to manage carrying my books, my satchel, and my lunch box. How did I do this since we didn't own a bus on the farm? Well, I took the 6 chairs from the dining table, arranged them in the living room in two rows with an aisle between. I used a footstool for the bus driver's seat. I would gather my gear and commence practicing getting onto the school bus. I would do this maybe 10 times each day just to make sure I got it right. I practiced looking for a vacant seat, and how I would kindly ask someone if I could sit next to them. I was the next-to-last stop so the bus was quite full by the time I got on it.

I would then practice getting off the bus. That was just as important as getting on, you know.

I heard somewhere that to master an ability, it has to be practiced 10,000 times. I didn't practice bus boarding quite that much, but I did feel more prepared when school started.

The act of practicing a skill does help us improve. When we are just learning how to do something such as play an instrument, sew, cook, or play a sport, we are not typically going to be very good at it. It's with practice and perhaps training that we improve.

When we decide to dedicate our lives as Christians, we may not be well versed in all there is to understand. We're not going to begin that walk knowing everything there is to know about God or our faith. We take baby steps and drink spiritual "milk" before we move on to the meat.

"I gave you milk, not solid food, for you were not yet ready for it." 1 Corinthians 3:2

The process of maturing is different for everyone, but we are expected to keep getting better and stronger.

"Let us move beyond the elementary teachings about Christ and be taken forward to maturity…"
Hebrews 6:1

Each day is a day to practice new skills in our faith. We will never perfect it, but we can certainly grow and improve. Just as an athlete or musician has a rough game or recital, we're going to have rough days too, where we make mistakes or "play the wrong note." The key is to be graceful to ourselves and keep working at it.

Hard Impact

Many of the kids in my first-grade class had been losing that first front tooth and started having those smiles with the big gaps. I would try to wiggle mine, but they were not even a tiny bit loose.

There were stories of strings tied and doors slammed. There were other tales of apples being eaten with a tooth left in the bite mark. I heard about a tooth fairy, too, who left money for every tooth lost!

About this time one of my front teeth started changing to a grayish color. This was not normal and it alarmed my mom. That's when I was told about a tumble that happened to me when I was very young; before I could hold memories. Somehow, I had fallen off our front porch and hit my mouth on the way down. To be more specific, I hit my left, front tooth; the one that was turning gray.

Mom set up an appointment with a dentist to have a look at it, and in a few days, I was experiencing my first dentist appointment. He looked at the discolored tooth carefully and took in the information that my mom shared about the fall from the porch that happened about five years earlier. The dentist surmised that damage had been done to the nerves from the impact, and that was causing the discoloring as the tooth began to loosen.

The tooth needed to come out, so the dentist pulled it that very day. The other kids in my class had bragged about losing their first tooth, but none of them had theirs pulled at the dentist! I was a bit nervous, but it was all over within a few minutes. Then the dentist presented me with a tiny, red, plastic, treasure chest. He lifted the lid and there was my tooth! Boy, oh, boy! I now had a "first lost tooth" story to tell my classmates and mine was completely different from all of theirs.

Well, the story didn't end there. As that permanent tooth came in, it didn't come in straight like my other teeth. It came in slightly angled and crooked. My smile was forever affected by that one fall.

Life is like that. One decision or one event can change the direction our life takes. Choices, even those out of our control, can reach far and wide and have long-lasting effects. Since choices are so impactful, it's vital to have a treasure chest full of jewels of wisdom, knowledge, and understanding. Here are a few to get you started:

"Blessed are those who find wisdom, those who gain understanding..." Proverbs 3:13

"If any of you lacks wisdom, you should ask God, who gives generously to all without finding fault, and it will be given to you." James 1:5

"I will instruct you and teach you in the way you should go; I will counsel you with my loving eye on you." Psalm 32:8

"The Lord makes firm the steps of the one who delights in him; though he may stumble, he will not fall, for the Lord upholds him with his hand." Psalm 37:23-24

We will never know how far and wide our influence will touch others. It might be positive or it could be negative, so it's up to us to gain and use wisdom.

Animal Hospital

My mom loved a clean house and twice a year she would give the whole house a good goin' over. She typically did this while we were at school.

All of the walls were wood paneling, and she would wipe down every wall in the house with a wood cleaning product.

She emptied all the cabinets, wiped them out, relined them with paper and then put everything back in place.

She washed all the curtains and cleaned all the windows inside and out.

She pulled the refrigerator away from the wall and cleaned out the dust that collected in that area. The refrigerator would be emptied and wiped out. Ice crystals would build up on the walls of the freezer and she would defrost it to keep the freezer running efficiently.

Furniture was moved to clean floors. Rugs were taken outside and shaken.

I feel tired just from thinking about all that cleaning!

Mom enjoyed surprising us too. So, one time after Mom had done her thorough cleaning, my sister and I came home from school to find our bedroom had been turned into an animal hospital! Our stuffed animals were stretched out over our bed and were covered in bandages.

"Create in me a pure heart, O God, and renew a steadfast spirit within me." Psalm 51:10

A clean home does renew us. I know Mom felt a sense of renewal when she got this task behind her.

A clean heart can feel good too. Pray for a renewed spirit, and removal of the unpleasant things that may be cluttering in there.

Sweet Tea

My dad was a hard-working man. He'd spend his
days working at our town's waterworks facility.
When he came home, he'd get busy with farming.
He'd get on his tractor and plant or plow, or harvest.

Imagine being on a tractor during the dry, hot
summer after already working all day at a tiring job.
The sun is still high and so are the temperatures.
You're sweaty. The dirt creates thick clouds of dust
around you as you're plowing through it. Sweat and
dirt collect on your skin and combine to create a
sticky mess that sits on your face, neck, and arms.

Imagine turning your tractor to go down another
row and you see a small figure walking toward you.
That small figure is one of your daughters. She's
been in the house helping Mom fix dinner, but dinner
isn't quite ready yet, and she's bringing you
something in her hands. You know what she has and

you will the tractor to move a little faster so you can meet her more quickly, or, you try to will her to move her legs more quickly because you know what she's carrying. In her hands is a nice, big, glass of sweet, iced tea. The tea will give some relief from the discomfort of the heat and will moisten your dry throat.

Sometimes I was the daughter carrying that glass of gold to my dad. I remember the glass getting slippery from the condensation, and I would be concerned about dropping it. I also didn't walk very fast because I was afraid I'd spill it.

When we got within a few feet of each other, Dad would slow his tractor to a stop and smile down at me. I'd reach up and he'd reach down to exchange that sweet glass of tea. He'd swallow it down in almost a single gulp. It was sweet relief.

(This little exchange was also code from my mom that dinner was almost ready and he needed to find a stopping point.)

Dad would make a couple more passes in the field and then come in for dinner.

One of the lessons Jesus wanted us to understand was that we need to take care of each other.

"If anyone gives even a cup of cold water to one of these little ones who is my disciple, truly I tell you, that person will certainly not lose their reward."
Matthew 10:42

"I needed clothes and you clothed me, I was sick and you looked after me, I was in prison and you came to visit me." Matthew 25:36

Simple stuff can mean so much.

Sweet, iced tea is a southern thing I'm told. I never acquired a taste for tea which causes many to question my southern roots.

Words

As I have mentioned, I was the baby of the family. My two siblings were a bit older than me, and they were my window to the world. I watched how they behaved and listened to what they said. I listened to their music and watched what they watched on tv. It really is true that we never know what kind of influence we have because I'm sure my siblings never had any idea how closely I watched them so I could mimic them. I was quite impressionable.

When I started school, my brother was in high school and my sister was in middle school. So, in my eyes, they had all the cool trends and attitudes. I remember hearing them speak certain phrases that I thought sounded hip and current. In fact, I thought they were so cool, I should learn how to use them in my everyday speech. I wanted to impress those around me with my knowledge and hipness.

I remember sitting at the dinner table one evening just waiting for an opportunity to use my most recently acquired catchphrase. I waited for just the right moment. Then, it happened! A place to fit my phrase into the family conversation. The adrenaline flowed as I spoke the phrase, and for a brief moment, I felt so "big"; so "grown-up"; so "hip." But the moment was met with a sharp attitude adjustment from my parents. I remember my pride fell quickly as I was rebuked and scolded for speaking in such a way.

I don't remember the phrase. I just remember the before and after of my words. Apparently, those words were sassy and shouldn't be coming out of my 6 or 7-year-old mouth. Whatever I said, I said in innocence, but it had repercussions.

This is a lesson I am still learning in my adult years. I say things, thinking it makes me look cute or funny, only to learn that my words aren't so cute and funny. I offend people sometimes or hurt their feelings.

The Bible gives us several scriptures about the words we say:

"Those who guard their mouths and their tongues keep themselves from calamity." Proverbs 21:23

"What goes into someone's mouth does not defile them, but what comes out of their mouths, that is what defiles them." Matthew 15:11

"Set a guard over my mouth, Lord; keep watch over the door of my lips." Psalm 141:3

"Even fools are thought wise if they keep silent, and discerning if they hold their tongues." Proverbs 17:28

While I may have been a little misguided in some of what I observed in my siblings, what I learned from them wasn't all bad…not at all. They showed me the model of how to obey and respect our parents. They showed me how to be helpful and kind to others. They taught me that family is about love. I looked up to them far more than they know. I'm thankful for their examples even still today because I'm still watching.

Cardboard Box

It's true that cardboard boxes are often the best toys. One summer while my brother was home from college, I remember him making a "car" for me out of a cardboard box. It was quite snazzy. He cut a door on one side and cut out the handle too. On the inside, he drew a steering wheel, a gear shifter, windshield wiper button, a button for headlights, and a glove compartment. He also drew in the gas pedal and the brake. But the best part, the VERY best part, was the 8-track tape player. Not very many cars had that luxury item, but mine did. He drew the slot and cut a flap so it looked like a real one. Then he made some 8-track tapes from matchboxes. He wrapped the matchboxes with masking tape and labeled them with names of bands or singers he enjoyed listening to. It was so cool!

I felt SO special because I was set to go cruising, wearing my sunglasses, while riding in my (cardboard) convertible, with that 8-track tape player blaring tunes.

Gadgets are fun and we can appreciate nice things like convertibles. There's nothing wrong with having nice things. Our motive for attaining them is what needs to be evaluated.

"Keep your lives free from the love of money and be content with what you have, because God has said, 'Never will I leave you; never will I forsake you'." Hebrews 13:5

God offers a contentment, a peace, that we won't find anywhere else.

"But godliness with contentment is great gain. For we brought nothing into the world, and we can take nothing out of it." 1 Timothy 6:6-7

My brother will probably be surprised that I remember that cardboard creation he fixed up for me. It wasn't the convertible or the 8-track tape player that made me feel so special. It was the thought and the effort that spoke love to me.

Bibles and Carrots

One of my early Bible school teachers had a rewards system for those of us who brought our Bibles to class and also if we knew our memory verse. She had little bookmarks and such for bringing our Bibles and she gave points when we said the memory verse. My Bible went to church with me every Sunday morning, and I had my memory verse memorized just long enough to get my prize. Eventually, I racked up enough points and "earned" the big prize which was a new, bigger Bible with my name on it. It had a white leather cover and my name was in gold letters.

Incentives can be used as a tool to encourage. I was certainly "encouraged" to make sure I had my Bible and memory verse ready each Sunday morning because I knew I would get a prize and more points from my teacher. There was also a bit of friendly competition with the other kids in that class. We tried to "one-up" each other and show off by comparing the points we had.

As I look back on this, though, I realize my heart was not really in it. My teacher put a carrot in front of me to push me a little, but I only wanted the reward my teacher had promised me. The memory work was not really memorized. I crammed it into my brain for a short while just so I could get my prize.

"Not everyone who says to me, 'Lord, Lord,' will enter the kingdom of heaven, but only the one who does the will of my Father who is in heaven." Matthew 7:21

"And without faith, it is impossible to please God, because anyone who comes to him must believe that he exists and that he rewards those who earnestly seek him." Hebrews 11:6

I encourage you to keep digging deeper. Instead of following the carrot, search for the true treasure that you can inherit.

"The kingdom of heaven is like a merchant looking for fine pearls." Matthew 13:45

Friends

Not many people can say they have a friend they've known all their life, but I can. Stephanie and I grew up in church together, and we are just a month apart in age. We knew each other from the nursery class all the way through high school. She and I would bring our baby dolls to church and take care of them together. We went to birthday parties together. We spent Sunday afternoons playing dress up or drawing together. Through our teen years, we both learned how to sew and we would admire each other's creations. We went to different schools, but church and common interests bonded us as friends.

I married my high school sweetheart just a few months after graduating high school, and I moved a long way from home because my husband was in the military. Stephanie and I were moving in different directions with our lives, and I had assumed that our childhood friendship would sort of stop there mainly because I had moved so far away.

I remember going to the mailbox on a very pretty fall day and there was a letter from Stephanie. That letter changed me. I realized that I was important to Stephanie and she wanted to stay connected with me. I felt so loved. I immediately wrote her back and this would continue for many years to come.

God made us to need each other. He made us a community so that we could be strong together. He knows how important it is to have support and encouragement because he made us that way. And just like we need each other, God pursues us to keep our relationship going with Him. He desires contact with us through prayer and using the Spirit to enrich our lives.

Stephanie and I don't get to see each other very often. We live in separate states and kids keep us busy. But when we do get together, it's like we've never been apart. We pick right back up where we left off.

"Therefore encourage one another and build each other up, just as in fact you are doing." 1 Thessalonians 5:11

Do you have a friend that needs encouragement? Maybe they just need to know someone cares. Let's stay connected, to our friends and to our Holy Father.

Playing Office

On the farm, there was paperwork that had to be managed and my mom was in charge of all that. I watched her pay bills and file papers. It all looked pretty important. It looked like office work.

My friend, Stephanie, and I loved playing "office" together. My "office" was set up in the closet under my hanging clothes. I had a little desk, some pens, and a receipt pad. Stephanie and I would shuffle papers back and forth, pay bills, and take phone calls for our make-believe boss. My prized possession was a date stamp. In my mind, I was a true secretary because I had that stamp. I could put dates and special marks on all my papers to make them official and bona fide. I knew official papers and documents were often marked with some sort of special seal or impression. I imagined I was one of the people in charge of putting the marks on them.

Scripture tells us that we have been marked with a special seal, too.

"And you also were included in Christ when you heard the message of truth, the gospel of your salvation. When you believed, you were marked in him with a seal, the promised Holy Spirit." Ephesians 1:13

"...He anointed us, set his seal of ownership on us, and put his Spirit in our hearts as a deposit, guaranteeing what is to come." 2 Corinthians 1:21-22

If that doesn't make you feel bona fide, I don't know what will.

Dressing Up

I loved playing dress up and pretending I was a grown up. I have pictures of friends coming over and spending Sunday afternoon doing that very thing with me. We would put on my sister's dresses, my mom's shoes and all kinds of jewelry. I remember in particular clip earrings that pinched and hurt my earlobes, but I wore them anyway because that's what grown-ups did. My sister fixed up our hair and put some makeup on our faces. Lipstick was the big deal. I remember little lipstick samples that Mom would have around and we would try every color. We filled our purses with pretend driver's licenses and fake money. We'd gather our baby dolls and off down the hall we would go pretending we were little mommies going to the store or to church. I can still hear the shuffling and scuffling sounds we made trying to walk in those shoes.

We were mimicking what we had seen modeled for us by our moms and other Christian women in our lives. We pretended we were wives, mothers, and Sunday school teachers. We would care for our babies, and teach our stuffed animals about God and Jesus. I pretended to walk a certain way because our preacher's wife had a quirky walk, and I wanted to be like her in every way.

Just as my friends and I imitated the women around us in our young years, Paul tells us to be imitators of God and Christ in our adult years.

"Therefore, be imitators of God, as beloved children; and walk in love, just as Christ also loved you." Ephesians 5:2 NASB

"Follow my example, as I follow the example of Christ." I Corinthians 11:1

I have to say my early Sunday school teachers made it look easy. My stuffed animals spoiled me with their good behavior. They were nothing like the real ones with working mouths, arms, and legs.

Family Portrait

Ah. The family portrait. The arrangement of the
family members. The perfect smiles. The favorite
outfit that took hours to pull together for the perfect
look. The perfect hair day...

(Do you hear the brakes screeching to a halt?)

No. The hair was not perfect, and that was what
had me so upset to the point of tears.

The photographer had set up shop in two adjoining
motel rooms. One room was the waiting room and
the other was where he was taking the pictures.
There were several other families in the waiting room
when we got there so we had to wait and wait even
though we had an appointment.

I had washed my hair before we left the house so
that it would look its best. I looked in the mirror

85

when we got to the motel and saw that my hair was not drying like it normally did. Disaster had struck; my hair was flipping out, not under. You see, I was a bit obsessive about my hair. There was a certain way it was supposed to look and if it didn't look that way, then my world was off-kilter; I didn't feel "right." Nothing I tried made my hair behave. I started crying which upset my mom because I would have red eyes in the picture. Oh no! Bad hair AND red eyes! The whole picture was going to be ruined because my hair wasn't doing what I wanted it to do.

There are some good scriptures to help get our perspective back in focus after we've flipped out (pun intended) over our appearance.

"Your beauty should not come from outward adornment, such as braided hair and the wearing of gold jewelry and fine clothes. Instead, it should be that of your inner self, the unfading beauty of a gentle and quiet spirit, which is of great worth in God's sight." 1 Peter 3:3-4

"The Lord said to Samuel, 'Do not consider his appearance...The Lord does not look at the things man looks at. Man looks at the outward appearance, but God looks at the heart." 1 Samuel 16:7

While it was a bit aggravating at the time, we did have quite a long wait to have our picture taken. I had time to accept the fact that my hair wasn't going to behave the way I thought it should, and my red eyes had time to go back to normal.

That portrait hung on the living room wall up to the last day my mom lived in that home. I didn't see my "flipped out" hair or any traces of tears. No. Instead, I saw a moment in time that represented my family; a family that loved each other, on good and bad hair days.

Expected Unexpecteds

I love getting mail. I always have. There is something about going to the mailbox, opening the door, and seeing what's inside. What will I find today?

When I was a young girl, there were a couple of companies that would entice customers to buy their products by sending fabric samples in the mail along with their brochures. These samples were polyester knits and only about 1 ½" X 2", and they would be different colors and textures. My sister would use them to make the tiniest doll clothes, and I do mean tiny. We had these little bitty dolls that had big heads and small bodies. My sister would make teensy weensy pants and tops for them to wear. They were SO cute. We learned to watch for these particular envelopes in the mail.

Another thing we looked forward to finding in the magic mailbox was the annual Christmas catalogs. Oh! The joy! It was almost like Christmas morning just getting the catalogs! How I loved looking through the pages pondering what I wanted for Christmas! Mom would instruct us to mark what we liked so Santa would know what to bring us, and I took this very seriously.

Both of these stories tell of expected unexpecteds. The fabric samples didn't come often, but they did come. We just didn't know when to expect them so it was a thrill when they did show up. It's the same thing with the Christmas catalogs. We knew they would come, but we didn't know for certain when they would show up. We just knew they would.

Anticipation. We wait and watch knowing something will happen...eventually. The time and day are unknown, but we know without a doubt that it will happen.

You know where I'm going with this...

"As it was in the days of Noah, so it will be at the coming of the Son of Man. For in the days before the flood, people were eating and drinking, marrying and giving in marriage, up to the day Noah entered the ark; and they knew nothing about what would happen until the flood came and took them all away. That is how it will be at the coming of the son of man." Matthew 24:37-39

"Therefore, keep watch, because you do not know the day or the hour." Matthew 25:13

We know Christ is coming. It's an expected unexpected. It should be thrilling to think of, but I wonder how many are filled with dread or fear at the thought. It's certainly something one should ponder. It will happen...eventually.

Dustin' and Cleanin'

To make a little extra money, my parents took on the role of janitors for our church. Every week, as a family, we would go clean the building. We each had responsibilities. Mom did the bathrooms and wet mopping, Dad and my brother did dust mopping and trash, and my sister vacuumed. Because I was the youngest, I was given the easiest task of cleaning the pews. I dusted them, cleaned out the songbook holders of any trash, and faced the songbooks in the correct, forward-facing direction. We worked as a team to accomplish the work and it was completed fairly quickly when we were all there to do our jobs.

As my siblings grew up and moved away, I took over their jobs. It took longer to get the work completed, too. It was more efficient when the jobs could be spread out over the whole family.

Paul wrote about teamwork in the church family.

"For just as each of us has one body with many members, and these members do not all have the same function, so in Christ we, though many, form one body, and each member belongs to all the others. We have different gifts according to the grace given to each of us." Romans 12:4-6

"Just as a body, though one, has many parts, but all its many parts form one body, so it is with Christ...Even so the body is not made up of one part but of many." 1 Corinthians 12:12, 14

Paul is explaining how different parts of a body have different abilities and tasks, but each one is important in their own way. No one is greater or lesser than the other, because all parts are vital.

Are you an ear who hears someone hurting? Are you a mouth that can speak hope? Are you a foot that can travel to other places to serve?

We all have something to offer. May God show you your talents and may you choose to use them for Him.

Small Town Living

One of the pros of living in a small town is everyone knows everyone. One of the cons of living in a small town is everyone knows everyone.

One of the ways we entertained ourselves out on the farm was to sit on the front porch and watch the traffic go by. When someone we knew drove by, they would honk and wave. We usually knew who it was by their vehicle. It was a busy road so there was a lot of honking and a lot of waving.

Yes, there were pros and cons to living in a small town. Folks were usually friendly to each other. Trips to the store might take a little longer due to friendly chit chat. If you ever had car trouble and had to pull off to the side of the road, you would probably know the next person that drove by and they would stop to help.

But sometimes it wasn't so nice and friendly. Everyone got into everyone else's business and rumors would swirl. Truths would become mangled and contorted into unrecognizable tales. Feelings would get hurt, and grudges would develop. When these things happened, it made small-town living uncomfortable.

Being a good neighbor is SO important. It's the second most important assignment we're given as Christians. When Jesus was asked what was the most important commandment of all, he said to love God with all your heart, soul, mind, and strength. The second was to love your neighbor as yourself (Mark 12:30-31). He said there was nothing more important than these two things.

Here are some other scriptures that can go along with being a good neighbor:

"Be devoted to one another in love. Honor one another above yourselves." Romans 12:10

"Love does no harm to a neighbor." Romans 13:10

"Be kind and compassionate to one another, forgiving each other, just as in Christ God forgave you." Ephesians 4:32.

"Above all, love each other deeply, because love covers over a multitude of sins." 1 Peter 4:8

Those times on our front porch were sweet. The sound of a car horn became synonymous with a warm hug. I knew those going by honking cared in some way about my family and me.

Heeding the Warning

My brother and I liked to rough house and wrestle. Sometimes the play would get a bit rowdy, and when things got rowdy...well...Mom would warn us, "Someone's gonna be cryin' in a minute." She was usually right, too. A head would get bonked or someone would get scratched. You know how it is.

The thing is, her warning didn't seem to keep us from continuing our roughhousing. We'd be laughing and scuffling and then, sure enough, someone would get hurt. Mom had much wisdom about what the scuffling could cause because she had seen it time and time again. Experience had taught her.

The Bible is full of advice and warnings. Proverbs, in particular, speaks highly of gaining wisdom and following that path.

"Pride goes before destruction, and a haughty spirit before a fall." Proverbs 16:18

Our little scuffles didn't seem destructive, nor did it seem there were haughty spirits involved. We scoffed at Mom's warnings and shrugged them off. After all, we were just playing around. Nothing was going to happen. No one was going to get hurt. Or so we thought. Yes, we thought we knew better. That's pride with a dash of haughty spirit.

I don't think we ever listened to Mom's warning when we started one of our wrestling matches. My mom's phrase would go a bit further as we got older. She would still say, "Someone's gonna be cryin' in a minute." She later added, "And it ain't gonna be me."

Crisp Fresh Sheets

Every Saturday we stripped our beds and washed our sheets. It was one of Mom's weekly routines. If the weather was favorable, Mom would hang our sheets on the clothesline in the back yard to dry in the wind and fresh air. I liked it when they were dried outside. The sheets would have a fresh crispness to them, and they smelled like sweet sunshine.

The word "fresh" makes me think of spring when everything starts coming back to life after a cold winter. It's a renewal; a new beginning; it feels hopeful.

When life brings challenges and hearts need refreshing, God offers a place of renewal where mercy and grace can wash through us. Once again, we can be filled with hope and made clean from the mistakes we've made. There is a deep comfort in knowing that we can have a new beginning; a fresh start.

"The steadfast love of the Lord never ceases; his mercies never come to an end; they are new every morning; great is your faithfulness."
Lamentations 3:22-23 (ESV)

Looking back, I realize Mom dried our laundry on that clothesline when she could to keep the electricity bill low. It never occurred to me then. It didn't matter. I only knew it put a smile on my face when it was time to go to bed on those Saturday nights. I sandwiched myself between those fresh sheets, laid my head on my soft pillow, said my prayer, and slept peacefully.

Dad's Keyring

I was fascinated by my dad's keyring. He had a keyring for work that was LOADED with keys. It was a silver, retractable keyring that he wore on his waistband for easy access. I loved to look at all the different keys he carried. They were all different shapes, sizes, and even colors.

I heard someone say that the number of keys you have shows how much responsibility you have. My dad was loaded.

"Whoever can be trusted with very little can also be trusted with much, and whoever is dishonest with very little will also be dishonest with much."
Luke 16:10

My dad was truly a trustworthy man.

One of the keys my dad used wasn't on his keyring because it was too big. This one was kept in his work truck. It was a large, gold-painted key. It was simple in structure to be used universally. This key wasn't for hiding or protecting anything. It was used to lift the lids on water-meter covers, and it made his work of reading water meters easier.

During the summer I would sometimes go out with Dad to help him read water meters. I was thankful for that lid key. If I didn't have it, I had to stick my finger down in the hole of the lid to lift it. I never knew what was going to be under that meter lid. The key provided a little distance between me and any critter that might be hiding in there.

The way to Christ is a universal key. Access to him is available to anyone.

"I am the gate; whoever enters through me will be saved." John 10:9

"I am the way and the truth and the life. No one comes to the Father except through me." John 14:6

It's ironic how a key that is so universal, is the one that gives the most riches. There is no dollar amount that can be given to the treasures we can find in a life with him. It is truly priceless.

Doing the Dishes

Cleaning up after dinner was a well-practiced ritual. Glasses were gathered and emptied in the sink. Plates were scraped and stacked with silverware on the top. Leftovers were put in containers and put in the refrigerator. Mom's lemon for her tea and the butter were also put in their proper spots in the refrigerator.

We didn't have a dishwasher. We washed the dishes in the kitchen sink. So, the order of washing was about the same as removing them from the table. Glasses were first, silverware second, and then you wiped down the countertop and the table. Next were the plates and bowls that held the food. After that, you could wash the pots and pans.

There were reasons for the order in which the dishes were washed. You wanted to do the glasses first so they didn't get any greasy residue. They would dry spotless. Silverware was next for the same reason; you didn't want greasy spots left on them either. Countertops and table were next because the water was still fairly clean. Plates and food bowls were a bit messy but not as bad as the pots and pans. Pots and pans were last because they were the messiest part of the cleanup. Sometimes the pots needed to soak before they could be cleaned thoroughly.

Because there was an order to cleaning the kitchen after a meal, it was easy to accomplish the task without leaving anything undone. It was a good thing. You might even say it's a Godly thing.

"For God is not a God of disorder, but of peace."
1 Corinthians 14:33

When things feel chaotic, it can be unsettling. With order comes peace and calm. God offers us peace as a fruit of His spirit. We should seek it and desire it in our lives.

Fear of Spiders

My fear of spiders began when I was very young because I do not remember a time not being afraid of them. I know it's an irrational fear because I am so much bigger than they are, but when I see one my brain tells me, "It's going to attack you! RUN!"

I remember a night when my sister and I were getting ready for bed. We pulled back the covers and there was a BIGGO spider hiding in the sheets! I don't think I slept well that night.

Another spider memory I have is of Mom on the kitchen floor getting ready to cut out a dress. She had the fabric laid out with her paper pattern neatly pinned. A big spider...covered with babies...found her way to the middle of Mom's project. Mom didn't want the babies to scatter so she put a glass over it and scooted some cardboard under it so it could be taken outside.

I get the heebie geebies just thinking about it.

As a child, I had awful nightmares about spiders, too. There's a part of one of those dreams I remember to this day! In my dream, I went out our back door and when I turned around to go back inside, the back of our house was covered with one giant spider. The legs stretched from one end of the house to the other and the body was the size of a car.

Fear is a natural emotion that God gave us, and it's actually a protection built into us. Fear is not always bad. But when a life circumstance comes along that is trying, our fear is a reflection of our trust in Him.

"There is no fear in love, but perfect love casts out fear because fear has to do with punishment."
1 John 4:18

Does perfect love mean perfect trust? If we could truly understand how much we are loved and treasured by God, then that alone should take away all our fears.

"For God did not give us a spirit of timidity, but of power, of love and of self-discipline." 2 Timothy 1:7

Being marked with the seal of the Holy Spirit should empower us and give us a deep and satisfying feeling of security.

"If God is for us who can be against us?"
Romans 8:31

God wants us to live boldly and courageously; not fearing trouble that may arise.

I still don't like spiders. There's something about those 8-legged critters that makes my skin crawl. To be courageous like God wants, I will try not to scream the next time I see one. I will try to boldly go to my husband and ask him to deal with it.

Numbers...Real and Imagined

My mom had a number she liked to use when she was feeling exasperated. It would go something like this:

"I've told you forty-leven times not to do that."

Forty-leven was a mixture of 40 and 11. It was a conjured-up silly number that made no sense, and she used it when it was necessary to exaggerate how many times she'd had to do something.

I remember us analyzing the number one evening in the kitchen as she was preparing dinner. We were both feeling quite silly. I said the number meant 51; 40+11. Or maybe it was 40 X 11. That would be 440. Whatever the reason was for her pulling that number out, you knew it represented "a lot."

In scripture, numbers were sometimes symbolic such as the number 7. It represented completeness. This number is used in a conversation in Matthew 18 where Peter is asking Jesus just how many times should he forgive someone. "Seven times?" he asks, thinking he's being complete in his forgiving. Jesus tells him, "...not just 7 times, but seventy-seven times." Peter was possibly feeling pretty generous about being willing to forgive someone 7 times. Then Jesus tells him that even seven is not complete enough.

What if God forgave us only 7 times? Or even 77 times? Or even 70 X 7? Where would that put you? The thought of that makes me appreciate the grace and mercy he gives me so much more. That was what Jesus was trying to emphasize; forgive others as God forgave and continues to forgive you...over and over and over again.

Stuck on Ice

It didn't snow often where I grew up. When it did, it was fun to go outside and observe how different the landscape looked covered in white fluff.

One of those times, I was walking near the edge of our field. There were tractor-tire ruts where water had frozen. I saw movement on one of these frozen puddles, and on closer inspection, I saw a bird whose wing was stuck to the ice. It was so scared. I gently pried it lose and took it inside. I figured it was nearly frozen to death after being stuck on the ice like that. My mom found a shoe box and we put the bird inside it to keep it from flying all over the house.

The little bird warmed up, it began to chirp and sing. My curiosity was bigger than my common sense, and I lifted the box lid to watch the little bird. Well, you know what happens when you open a cage; whatever is inside escapes. That little bird flew out of the box and all over the living room flitting from one spot to the next. I yelled out to my mom, and she came running. I had to admit to her that I had accidentally let the bird out, but she didn't get angry with me. She just stood there trying to figure out how in the world we were going to get that bird outside. We finally decided to work together to shoo it out the door. I would hold the door open while mom would guide it in that direction. It worked! We had managed to get it out.

There is a story in Acts 16 about Paul and Silas being in jail. They were locked up in the dungeon and their feet were put in stocks. They were not going anywhere. In the night, they started singing and praying, and the other prisoners listened. There was a massive earthquake that caused the prison doors to be opened and the chains fell off of all the prisoners. For some reason, Paul, Silas and all the other prisoners didn't leave. The description seems to say they stayed in their cells. But when the guard saw the doors wide open, he assumed they had all escaped and he would be killed for not doing his job properly. So, as he was about to kill himself, Paul shouted to let him know they were all still there. The jailer was convicted in his heart that this had been an act of God and immediately asked Paul and Silas what he needed to do to be saved...to belong to God.

In fact, he and his whole family were baptized that very night.

It appears that God was rescuing Paul and Silas, but He also rescued the jailer and his family.

Southern Snow

Yes, snow was a rare event in the south. When snow was predicted, it was a race to the grocery store to stock up on milk and bread. (Still is…) There was no equipment available to clear the roads, so if it was a big snow, you may be stuck at home for several days.

I remember a particularly bad snow storm. It was Sunday morning and it was decided we needed to at least try to get to worship. We were the ones in charge of getting the doors open and the heat turned on at the church building. The roads were covered where we lived out away from town but thought it might be different in town. Dad was concerned folks would be making their way to the church building despite the bad roads.

My sister and I put on layers and layers of stockings, socks, turtlenecks, and sweaters. On this particular day, pants would be allowed. (Pants for girls going to worship were frowned on at this particular time in history.) We wrapped scarves around our necks and even layered gloves and mittens. It was probably the closest thing to a blizzard I had ever known. It was extremely cold and the snow piled up into big snow drifts that were probably four or five feet tall in places.

I remember moving at a snail's pace down the highway as Dad tried to drive through the snow. It was nearly impossible to tell where the road was and where the ditches were because the snow made it all look level. I don't think we got even a half mile down the road before Dad decided we needed to turn around and go back home; it was not safe to be out.

My dad had a deep sense of responsibility to our congregation. He wanted to make sure all was ready for anyone who came to worship that day. It was that important to him...because God was that important.

"And let us consider how we may spur one another on toward love and good deeds, not giving up meeting together, as some are in the habit of doing, but encouraging one another — and all the more as you see the Day approaching." Hebrews 10:24-25

Trains That Fade into the Background

Along the back part of our farm, there was a railroad track. Trains came all hours of the day and night. You could often feel the trains before you heard them. They had a certain rumble. As the train got closer you would hear the clickity-clack of the wheels rolling along the metal track. Then, as they approached where the highway and the railroad intersected, the red lights would flash their warnings along with the bells that would ding. The sigh of the train's whistle would come in long, loud bursts.

Since we lived near the track, the sounds and rumbles were normal, and we didn't really notice them that much. It seems kind of crazy to think that something as big as a train that makes a lot of noise and shakes the ground can go unnoticed, but for us, they faded into the background.

Just as the trains became fairly unnoticed to us, Jesus shares a thought with some people about how they've become blind to their own wrongdoings:

"Why do you look at the speck of sawdust in your brother's eye and pay no attention to the plank in your own eye?" Matthew 7:3

You would think a huge plank of wood wouldn't be missed, but how often I have done this very thing. I have been pretty nit-picky about what I saw in someone else when if I had just looked at myself, I would have seen not just a plank in my eye, but possibly a whole forest.

I'm thankful for the insight in this scripture. It reminds me that I always need humility and compassion for others.

On warm, sunny days, I would take walks on that back side of our property. When a train would come, I would stand there watching it whiz by and be in awe of the rumbling of the ground as this mighty machine sped past me. I would watch for the end, and when I saw it coming, I would jump up and down waving to the man sitting in the caboose. He usually waved back with a smile.

Clipped Wings

It was springtime and I was in fifth grade. Believe it or not, there was another Ida in my class back in the late 1970s. She brought some baby ducks to school one day and they were so cute! She said they had more to sell if I wanted some.

Well, I went home that day and told my mom and dad about these precious baby ducks, and that they were only $1 each. They discussed it and said, "Ok." I could have two.

Mom helped me figure out how I was going to transport these 2 little creatures from school to our house. I had a yellow, plastic picnic basket that would fit the bill (pun intended). It had a plastic lid with holes in it, and plastic cups where I could keep water in there for the babies all day at school. This would work, and I managed just fine getting those babies home.

My cute baby ducks grew up and out of the baby stage. They soon were full-fledged birds.

One evening my parents came to me saying that they thought it would be a good idea to "clip their wings". I felt such terror in my heart! WHAT?? CLIP THEIR WINGS?? I cried and begged Mom and Dad not to do it because that sounded like it would hurt them. They listened to my pleas and agreed not to do anything to the wings.

A few days later, my dad was drying off his face after his morning shave and happened to look out the bathroom window. He saw a huge bird flying in the sky out over the field. He realized it was one of my ducks. The duck flew out of his range of view, and he frantically went to another room to see where the duck went. The poor thing landed on the highway and was struck by a car.

A couple of days after that as I was catching the bus, the other duck took flight and chose to land...
on my leg...
as I was stepping onto the bus!

Its claws dug into my calf and its wings were flapping and hitting the bus doorway. My arms were full of books, and I tried to shake it off, but I could NOT get the duck to let go of my leg!

To better help you see this whole image, I must remind you that traffic laws say all vehicles must stop when a school bus is stopped. The traffic was stopped in both directions, and the cars were lining up as this drama played out. Lots of people were on their way to work at this time of day.

The duck did finally let go of my leg and plopped down on the shoulder of the road and just stood there. I got seated and, my bus driver asked me if I'd like to take my duck back to the house. Of course, that would be the right thing to do. I couldn't just leave him there on the side of the road.

Remember, traffic is stopped…in both directions.

So, I set down my books, and in my embarrassment, stepped off the bus and picked up my pitiful, lonely duck and carried him back to his pen.

After this incident, my parents explained what they meant about "clipping the wings." It would be a slight trimming of the wing feathers to keep the duck from being able to fly. My parents were only trying to protect them.

Paul wrote in Galatians 5:13 that "You…were called to be free. But do not use your freedom to indulge the flesh…"

I have free will and am allowed to make my own choices.

1 Corinthians 10:23 Paul says, "'I have the right to do anything,' you say, but not everything is

beneficial. 'I have the right to do anything,' but not everything is constructive."

As a child of God, He may not physically clip my wings, but He does want me to listen to the wisdom He offers. It is for my protection. There are many dangers out there that He wants me to avoid.

My duck sure caused a scene. I can just hear someone who was in that stopped traffic stepping into their workplace that morning saying, "Y'all are not going to believe what I saw on my way to work this morning..."

Projectors

You knew it was going to be a good school day when the teacher pulled out the movie projector. I remember watching with awe as my teacher would thread the film through slots and around knobs eventually connecting the film to an empty reel. It was a delicate process. The film could break so she did this with extreme care. Whoever was closest to the light switch had the privilege of darkening the room and would watch with intense focus for the teacher's cue to turn the lights off. My teacher would flip the machine on, and the projector motor would engage. The film would make a clicking sound as it wove through the mechanics of the projector. The light passed through each tiny frame and allowed each minute image from the film to come to life on the screen

We, as Christians, are like that projector. The Bible tells us to project a Christ-like image.

"You are the light of the world. A town built on a hill cannot be hidden. Neither do people light a lamp and put it under a bowl. Instead, they put it on its stand, and it gives light to everyone in the house. In the same way, let your light shine before others, that they may see your good deeds and glorify your Father in heaven." Matthew 5:14-16

Yes, be a light to the world. We're all telling a story by how we're living.

The Biggest Gift

My mom was a creative gift wrapper, especially at Christmas. One year she wrapped our gifts in the comics from the newspaper. Another year she found ornaments that were boxes and she hid little goodies in there for my sister and me. One year she gave my sister, sister-in-law, and me each a stuffed animal. I thought this was really weird because we were older, and we were too old to be receiving toys. Then she told us to look at the ears. To our surprise, she had put diamond earrings on the little animal's ears!

There's one Christmas that really stands out in my memory. My brother, sister and I woke up Christmas morning to a HUGE gift in front of our Christmas tree. The gift was almost as tall as the Christmas tree itself! I wondered which sibling it was for; my brother or my sister. They were older so it was obviously for one of them. The mystery continued because there was no name on it saying whose it was. But none of the other presents under the tree had my name on them. I started fearing that Santa had seen me misbehave and I hadn't received any gifts.

After some confusion and a little bit of worry, someone said that the big one was for me. That gift was for ME?? I'm sure my eyes were as big as saucers, and my mouth was as wide as the Mississippi River. I was in complete shock. Santa hadn't seen anything and I was feeling pretty special.

Once the shock wore off, I tore into that massive box to see what Santa had brought me. I was able to get the wrapping paper off, but the box was so tall I wasn't able to see what was inside. I had to have help to get it down on my level. Inside that massive box, was a big, yellow bean-bag chair. Wow! A bean-bag chair! But there was more! At the bottom of that big box were other individually wrapped gifts. "Santa" was pretty creative.

Yes, I was mighty surprised when they told me that gift was mine. I didn't think that gift was for me because I didn't think I was worthy of such a gift. Why would I get such an epic present!? My brother and sister were so much more deserving than me, right? (just because they were older...)

No, I didn't feel worthy.

There is another huge gift that we often have a difficult time realizing is for us; the gift of grace. Now THAT is a big gift.

"For it is by grace you have been saved, through faith—and this not from yourselves, it is the gift of God..." Ephesians 2:8

I didn't feel worthy of the big gift in front of our Christmas tree, but the gift of grace is not a matter of us being deserving because we will never be worthy or deserving of such a special gift. It can't be bought. It can't be earned. It's there for us to simply accept.

Paul writing about the gift of grace in 2 Cor 9:15 said, "Thanks be to God for His indescribable gift."

Spooky

Like most farms, we had cats around. They were there to keep the varmint population down. One of the cats we had was a black cat named Spooky.

Our cats spent the majority of their time outside, but we always let them come in to eat first thing in the morning, and they were usually waiting at the door meowing their little heads off begging to be let in for their morning meal.

One spring morning, Spooky wasn't there to greet us like he usually was. We searched and called for him, but he didn't show up. It wasn't that unusual for a cat (especially a male) to be gone for a day or two so we didn't think much about it. But after a couple of days, we got concerned. We walked the field calling and looking for him, but there was no sign of him. After a few days of this, we just assumed the worst; that he was truly gone for good and we'd never see him again. Those things happened.

Spring turned into summer and summer turned into fall. A new school year had begun. I usually sat by the kitchen door to watch for the bus, but this particular morning, I was not in my usual morning post. I was outside because it was a beautiful morning with the sun shining and a bright, blue, autumn sky. I had to stay focused on my bus watching. If I missed the bus I'd be in trouble. It was hard to stay focused though. My eyes wandered around the field as I sat there waiting. I looked out toward the back of our field and noticed something moving. It was something black. I looked back to where I would see the bus so I wouldn't miss it. I looked back to see the thing that was moving. It was still there and still moving...toward the house! I'd glance back to make sure the bus wasn't coming, but my attention was definitely on this thing in the field. Was it a dog? It didn't move like a dog. Maybe it was a cat. Lo and behold! It was a cat! I started calling, "Kitty! Kitty! Kitty!" and it came running! I hollered at Mom that there was a cat coming and it looked like Spooky! She came bounding out the door and by this time he was in the yard. He was meowing and purring and he was so happy to see us.

One of the parables Jesus told is recorded in Luke 15:4-7, and it's about a lost sheep.

"Suppose one of you has a hundred sheep and loses one of them. Doesn't he leave the ninety-nine in the open country and go after the lost sheep until he finds it? And when he finds it, he joyfully puts it on his shoulders and goes home. Then he calls his friends and neighbors together and says, 'Rejoice with me; I have found my lost sheep.' I tell you that in the same way there will be more rejoicing in heaven over one sinner who repents than over ninety-nine righteous persons who do not need to repent."

There was definitely some rejoicing going on in our yard that morning. I couldn't believe after all these months, Spooky had returned! Where had he been? Had he been staying with another family? I wished he could talk so he could tell us all about his adventures.

But I had to get back to watching for the bus. I did not want to go to school (read that with a slight whiney tone to understand what I'm saying here). Our sweet cat had returned and I just wanted to spend time with him. This was going to be a long school day.

My Big Adventure

During the summer between eighth and ninth grade, I went to visit my sister. She lived near St. Louis and was expecting her first child. The plan was Mom and Dad would take me there over a weekend, and then I would ride a bus back home the next week.

I had a really nice visit with my sister that week. It was the week of July 4th and we went to see the fireworks show. We shopped and watched tv. She worked on a sewing project for the baby's room. She and her husband were talking about baby names and I remember the very conversation at the dinner table when it was decided what their first child would be named. That was pretty special.

All week I was anxiously anticipating my return trip home; my big adventure. I was barely 14 and I was going on a big trip by myself. It was quite thrilling. My sister took me to the bus station early that day, and we said our goodbyes. I got on the bus and found a seat next to a couple of older ladies. They saw that I was traveling alone and assured me they would help me if I needed anything.

I had a bag filled with things to keep me occupied for the long trip home. I had a word-search book, some cross-stitching, and a crochet project too. I enjoyed switching from one project to the other as we journeyed along.

The bus stopped for lunch at a little café. Those sweet ladies made sure that I had money for food (I did), and that I was able to get my order placed. They were quite alarmed to see that I only ordered French fries. I tried to explain that I was a picky eater, and I only ordered French fries whenever I went to a restaurant. They were concerned I'd get hungry again. I told them I would be fine, this was standard procedure for me.

With our bellies full, we loaded back up on the bus and we were off again. The next stop would be home. This trip hadn't been difficult. That was never a concern. Doing this on my own was what made it so adventurous.

When we got close to my hometown, I let the ladies know that I would be getting off soon. They complimented me on how well I had managed and taken care of myself.

My dad was waiting for me at the bus stop. My big adventure had come to an end. I felt exhilarated and hoped I could do that again someday. This made me feel like I had accomplished something monumental.

"Don't let anyone look down on you because you are young, but set an example for the believers in speech, in conduct, in love, in faith, and in purity."
1 Timothy 4:12

Spread Thin

In my freshman year of high school, I wanted to be involved in everything. I was in choir. I was part of FHA (Future Homemakers of America). I joined the Thespians and got a role in the play that would be performed that fall. I had been in band, but I couldn't fit band into my school schedule. So, I worked it out with the director to do band after school in my own time.

Yes, I wanted to do it all and be a part of everything. My days during that time looked like this:

I got up at 6:30, caught the bus at 7:30, went through my classes all day and school released at 3:30. Then it was off to band practice and play rehearsal that sometimes lasted until 8:00 or 9:00 at night. Whatever homework I had for my classes, I squeezed in where I could. Many nights during that time I didn't get home until 9:00 or 9:30 at night. I was having the time of my life. This all went on for about 6 weeks.

And then I crashed. I was physically and emotionally exhausted. I couldn't go one more step.

It was Friday night and I was to march with the band that evening during halftime of the football game. My mom put her foot down and told me to call the band director and tell him I would not be able to make it. So, I did what she said. His response was, "You do what you have to do and I'll do what I have to do." It sounded like he understood and I was relieved.

Monday morning as I was going to my locker to get my day going, I was met by a group of my friends saying, "Ida Mae, did you know Mr. M kicked you out of band?"

What?? WHAT??? But I called him and explained myself. I thought it was all fine. Was there some sort of misunderstanding? I was in one of the most confused states I have ever experienced. I went to Mr. M asking if this was true. Oh, it was true alright, and he seemed all too happy to tell me I needed to turn in my uniform.

I was so hurt and disappointed. I thought I had handled things the right way. I called him as my mom told me, and I thought things were fine. How could he be doing this? After all, I was volunteering my time to be a part of our school's tiny band.

But...

Ultimately, I was to blame for my dismissal. I had tried to do too much and be too many things. I was squeezing too many activities into my days and it caught up with me.

You see, our band was very small, and with just one member absent, it made an impact on the performance. It wasn't respectful of the other band members either, because they worked hard to do their part. Mr. M had to let me go because if he let me get by with not showing up, how many other members would think it was ok to miss? He had to set the standard, even though it hurt me.

"Do nothing out of selfish ambition or vain conceit. Rather, in humility value others above yourselves, not looking to your own interests but each of you to the interests of others." Philippians 2:3-4

I have shared this story through the years, and I have told it from an attitude of pride because I didn't think I deserved my punishment. After all, I was sacrificing my time to benefit the band. But in actuality, I was being quite selfish by trying to be involved in so many activities. I was trying to prove my value to others by saying, "Look at what all I can do."

"Be careful not to practice your righteousness in front of others to be seen by them. If you do, you will have no reward from your Father in heaven." Matthew 6:1

That's a pretty serious warning and one to be thoughtful of when we're determining our commitments.

Recipe

I'm not a kitchen gal. I often feel like I'm just in the way when I'm in the kitchen with others, and most times I am. It's an awkward place for me to be.

I remember trying to learn how to make fudge. I had sort of seen my sister make it so all I had to do was follow a recipe, right?

I had just gotten home from school, and I dug through my mom's green, tin recipe box that she kept in the cabinet. I found a recipe that said "fudge" at the top. This was the only one I could find so it had to be the one my sister had used. I looked at the hand-written ingredients listed on the index card. There was an ingredient that I had seen my sister use, but it wasn't listed on this recipe. I was confused, but I began measuring and mixing everything together anyway. I measured out sugar...LOTS of sugar. I added some cocoa powder, butter, and some milk. I started heating this mixture on the stove, but what about that gooey, white marshmallow cream that my sister used? I knew she had used it so I decided to add it to the mix, too, even though it wasn't listed on the recipe card.

After a while, this chocolate mix was supposed to start setting up. I stirred and I stirred, but it didn't do anything. It just stayed goopy. I was getting frustrated. This wasn't turning out as I expected.

Mom came home from work and I told her my dilemma. She started asking me what I had mixed together and I told her. I told her the recipe didn't call for the marshmallow cream, but since my sister had always used it, I thought it needed to be added. That's when I learned how important it is to follow a recipe, and I shouldn't add ingredients that weren't listed.

How often do we live our lives like this? Instead of following God's instructions, we just start adding a little bit of "this" because we saw someone else do it. We add a little bit of "that" because we think it's a good idea. We might save ourselves some frustration if we'd learn to follow the recipe.

Jesus said in John 15:5 "I am the vine; you are the branches. If you remain in me and I in you, you will bear much fruit; apart from me you can do nothing."

Well, apart from that recipe, I couldn't make fudge. That is the truth.

I told Mom I had looked for the fudge recipe in her recipe box; one that called for the marshmallow cream, but I couldn't find it. She then showed me where to look. The correct recipe was on the **jar** of the marshmallow cream. Sometimes we should ask for help when we're attempting to broaden our horizons.

Threat at the Door

Our house was on a busy road, and every now and then we would get a knock on the door at night. It would be a stranded motorist who had run out of gas, or their car had broken down and they needed to use the phone. We usually knew them, and they were allowed to come in and call whoever they needed for help. Most folks were very appreciative and once the call was made, they were out the door with smiles of relief.

Not all who came knocking were allowed inside.

I remember one evening Mom was washing dishes and I was drying them. There was a knock at the door and my dad answered it. There was a young man asking if he could come in and use the phone. I saw my mom stealthily move a visible ice pick out of sight. Some type of warning bell was going off in her head and she sensed danger.

It would never have occurred to me that someone might come posing as someone in distress just so they could come inside to attack or case the place out to see what they might come back later to steal. No, that would never have crossed my mind until I saw my mom move that ice pick.

Jesus put out a warning about people with nefarious plans and schemes in the church.

"Watch out for false prophets. They come to you in sheep's clothing, but inwardly they are ferocious wolves." Matthew 7:15

These kinds of people are often able to fool even strong believers. They use their charm and persuasiveness to emotionally attach themselves to unsuspecting people. Then they subtly start twisting truths and they start a following that could tear a church in two.

The sad truth is that even the wolf doesn't realize they are a wolf. They convince themselves they speak truth.

Don't be caught spiritually naïve. Be aware of how the spiritual battle is being fought and don't let your guard down. Use the armor God provided to ward off any attack that may be on the other side of the door of your heart. The threat at the door is real.

Storms on the Horizon

The land was flatter than a pancake in the farming community where I grew up. It was perfect land for farming rice. The land was open, and you could see the horizon all the way around with almost no obstructions.

During the summer, I remember intense, dark and ominous skies when storms loomed on those horizons. I could see fingers of lightning stretching down to the ground or watch them branch out like limbs on a tree. The rumbles of their thunder could be heard and felt well before the storm arrived. They were the warning of what was coming.

I didn't like storms. They were unpredictable and frightening. I had heard stories of tornados and people losing their homes or their lives. I carried a lot of anxiety on my back when storms started peeking their dark heads over the edge of our town.

We were taught to gather flashlights and hunker down in a central part of our house when these threats came near. We would have pillows and blankets available to cover ourselves from possible debris should the storm brew up a tornado. I can still see my dad standing at the door watching the storm while we sheltered in the hallway. It filled me with fear seeing him standing there. I didn't want him there. I wanted him in the hallway with me so he wouldn't get hurt.

The wind would whistle and howl around the house. Gusts of wind would beat on the exterior walls and huff against the windows. Sometimes hail would ting, peck, or pound on the windows. It would seem like the intensity would have no end, but then the wind would quieten down. The rain would lighten up to a trickle. It would be over in a few short minutes.

Storms hit in life. Maybe they are visible on the horizon, and there is time to prepare for them emotionally, mentally, and spiritually. Or, maybe they aren't showing signs of arrival, and they hit at full force without warning.

If a storm of life were to hit today, warned or not, how would you handle it? Would you turn and run thinking you could get away from it? Or would you face the wind and rain head on with your feet firmly planted in God's solid ground?

It's best to prepare ahead of time for an emergency. To prep for a life storm, ask God for strength and courage, for wisdom and clarity, so that when life's storms hit, you can be strong and ready.

"Be on your guard; stand firm in the faith; be courageous; be strong." 1 Corinthians 16:13

After a storm passed over the farm, we would go outside to assess if there was any damage. Rain would still be falling as the clouds headed on to the east. The sun would smile on the raindrops, and a bright, beautiful rainbow would drape over the land. We could see it stretch from side to side; sometimes so bright it would reflect itself into a double rainbow.

In my personal experiences, whenever I've gone through a storm, there are blessings on the other side that I could never have imagined. It's in those moments of reflection I can see God had me braced. I chose to lean into him, and he gave me what I needed to get through it. When the next storm hits, I'll be even stronger, and I will look for the rainbow of blessings on the other side.

Critiques

I love to sew. My family heritage is rich with women who quilted and made clothing. I even had a great aunt who was a tailor. I remember visiting her and she would tell stories of her customers from all over the United States. It was fascinating to me.

I began taking a real interest in sewing when I was in high school. There was a sewing contest that I entered every year. The garment had to be made from 100% cotton; the thread, the interfacing, it all had to be 100% cotton. The first year I went was a learning experience because I really didn't know how this all worked. There were 3 different categories; evening wear, casual, and dressy.

I remember being in a room where all the contestants lined up around the wall and we waited our turn to be judged. The judges looked at each one of us in our garments. We were judged on fit, construction, and style. I remember looking around the room and sizing up who I thought would be the winners. The winners were eventually posted and it was no shocker that I didn't win, but what I learned from the critique they gave was truly valuable. I knew I would return again with a better chance.

The second year I competed, I decided to compete in the evening wear category. I made a rather fashionable dress from white, polished cotton. I had learned the previous year that the judges wanted the construction to be extremely neat and tidy, so I was determined to do all steps to the best of my ability. The dress itself wasn't too complicated. It had a decorative folded fabric design on the front, but it was mainly pleated and I knew I could do that easily. But the dress had a zipper down the back. I hadn't put in very many zippers at this point in my sewing experience. That zipper gave me some trouble and I don't know how many times I had to rework it to get it lined up correctly at the top. My white polished cotton didn't look so sharp and neat when I finally got the zipper sewn correctly. I tried to clean that one area at the top of the zipper because it had become slightly smudged from all my handling. The fabric had lost its sheen too. I couldn't do anything about it though. I just hoped it wouldn't be noticed.

The day of judging arrived. The sizing up began and I thought I might actually have a chance to place. It was my turn to be looked over. The judges looked closely at the work on the front and seemed impressed. Then they wanted to see the backside. I was hoping they wouldn't notice the rough spot. They asked questions as they judged. One of the questions they asked me was what was the hardest part of constructing this garment. Of course, I had to be honest and tell them the zipper. I felt one of them touching that top spot and saying that they could see that I had had some difficulty. I felt deflated. They had seen the smear and the area that was dulled by all my handling. I still had hope though. Maybe the other girls had stuff messed up on their garments too. Maybe...

When the judging was completed, we all clamored to the board where the winner-list was posted. No, my name wasn't there. When I got my critique back, I saw that the zipper was probably what kept me out of placing.

The next year I competed a third time. I had taken a risk by entering the evening wear competition with corduroy pants and a tuxedo-style blouse. I didn't really know how my garment would be received by the judges, but I knew it was constructed extremely well. The critiques I had received in previous competitions had helped me hone my skills and I knew what the judges would be looking for.

So much learning and growing came from these experiences, and I love reliving these times and telling my kids about them. These moments truly shaped me and made me better on several levels.

Our Christian walk isn't a competition, but God loves to develop character in His kids. He does this by putting us through all sorts of different situations. We don't really go through a critique as we live our lives, but there have been times when someone came to me and gently corrected me when I was in error. I'm thankful for those people. I'm thankful for the way God used them in my life and the love they showed me. It didn't always feel like love. Truth can hurt. But I was shaped into a better person because of their correcting.

"Blessed is the man who perseveres under trial, because when he has stood the test, he will receive the crown of life that God has promised to those who love Him." James 1:12

So how did I do in that last competition? I actually came in second place in my division. I was so excited and so encouraged. All the information I had gained through the years had helped me grow and improve.

After the competition, the winners were to put on a fashion show for the company that sponsored the contest. My brother was there because he worked for that company and this was their annual convention. He didn't realize I was there. He was sitting in the audience and was completely shocked when he heard his little sister's name being announced and saw me walking out on the stage as a contest winner. After the show, he came and found me and started telling me how he told everyone sitting around him that I was his little sister. He was proud of me and I was happier about *that* than winning the contest.

Past, Present, Future

I'm thankful for memories. Going back through my childhood and early years has been enriching. I realize that I was truly loved not only by my family but by many others. I had special teachers in my life. My parents and siblings were my first teachers. I'm so grateful that I was raised in a Christian home. I had aunts, uncles, and cousins who also played roles in shaping who I am. My school teachers and my Sunday school teachers touched my life in significant ways. My close friends also made impressions on me. There are many others who were just people in my life that had no idea I was looking to them for guidance. I could probably fill a whole book with just the names of people who taught me something.

Traveling through these pages of memories, I realized God was there through every minute of every day. His spirit was working through others to shape me into who I am now. I also know and accept that He is with me now as I live my life currently. He still works through others shaping me to be better and stronger. I can even see times when He uses me to help others. I find immense comfort in knowing He is also in the future. I don't know what is there, but He does, and I know He will be there to walk me through whatever is on my path.

It is my hope that you will embrace this knowledge, truth, and wisdom, and be comforted.

"The Lord your God is with you, He is mighty to save. He will take great delight in you, He will quiet you with His love, He will rejoice over you with singing." Zephaniah 3:17

Acknowledgements

First, I would like to give credit to Holy God for planting the seed that soon became a sprout and now a completed book to share with others.

I would like to thank my family for pouring out encouragement during this process.

I would like to thank my friends who kept fertilizing my determination with love and support as this project grew.

About the Author

Ida Mae is a farm-raised gal originally from Arkansas, who now resides in Tennessee. She grew up in a Christian home where she was given her deep foundation in Christ. She married her high school sweetheart and they have two wonderfully talented kids. She enjoys teaching Bible classes and sharing her love of sewing with other women.

To see photos from these stories, visit:

Instagram

@lobrypublishing

9 780578 474885